Ariana Grande

by **Sarah Tieck**

Big Buddy Books

An Imprint of Abdo Publishing
www.abdopublishing.com

www.abdopublishing.com

Published by Abdo Publishing, a division of ABDO, PO Box 398166, Minneapolis, Minnesota 55439.
Copyright © 2015 by Abdo Consulting Group, Inc. International copyrights reserved in all countries. No part
of this book may be reproduced in any form without written permission from the publisher. Big Buddy Books™
is a trademark and logo of Abdo Publishing.

Printed in the United States of America, North Mankato, Minnesota.
092014
012015

THIS BOOK CONTAINS
RECYCLED MATERIALS

Cover Photo: Getty Images.
Interior Photos: ASSOCIATED PRESS (pp. 7, 19); Getty Images (pp. 17, 22, 29); FRANK MICELOTTA/INVISION/
    AP (p. 15); NBC NewsWire via Getty Images (p. 13); Shutterstock.com (pp. 9, 13); Jordan Strauss/Invision/AP
    (pp. 5, 21); Charles Sykes/Invision/AP (p. 25); WireImage (pp. 11, 27).

Coordinating Series Editor: Rochelle Baltzer
Contributing Editors: Bridget O'Brien, Marcia Zappa
Graphic Design: Maria Hosley

Library of Congress Cataloging-in-Publication Data

Tieck, Sarah, 1976-
  Ariana Grande : famous actress & singer / Sarah Tieck.
    pages cm. -- (Big buddy biographies)
  ISBN 978-1-62403-568-5
1. Grande, Ariana--Juvenile literature. 2. Singers--United States--Biography--Juvenile literature. 3. Actresses--United
States--Biography--Juvenile literature. I. Title.
  ML3930.G724T54 2015
  782.42164092--dc23
  [B]
                    2014026415

Contents

Rising Star 4

Family Ties 6

Music Lover 8

Starting Out. 10

On Broadway 12

Lights! Camera! Action! 14

Break Out 18

Pop Singer. 20

A Performer's Life 23

Off the Stage 26

Buzz 28

Snapshot 30

Important Words 31

Websites. 31

Index 32

Ariana's first album is *Yours Truly.*

Rising Star

Ariana Grande is a talented actress and singer. She has appeared in television shows and movies. She is known for starring in *Sam & Cat*. Ariana has also released hit songs.

Alabama   Georgia

ATLANTIC OCEAN

Florida

GULF OF MEXICO

Boca Raton

Where in the World?

N
W   E
S

Family Ties

Ariana's full name is Ariana Grande-Butera. Ariana was born in Boca Raton, Florida, on June 26, 1993. Her parents are Joan Grande and Edward Butera. Her older half-brother is Frankie.

Ariana is part of a close family. In 2011, she went to a show opening with her grandfather Frank Grande, her mother, her half-brother, and her grandmother Marjorie Grande.

Music Lover

Boca Raton is on the Atlantic Ocean.

Ariana grew up near the beach. When she was eight, she began acting in a community theater. She got the starring **role** in the **musical** *Annie*.

Ariana continued acting, but she also enjoyed music. She listened to Whitney Houston and Judy Garland. Soon, she began making songs on her computer. She also played the French horn.

Did you know...

Ariana got ideas for songs from listening to music by Mariah Carey and Imogen Heap.

Starting Out

Over time, Ariana became more serious about **performing**. She began singing and dancing for larger audiences. In 2001, Ariana sang "The Star-Spangled Banner" for a Florida Panthers game. In 2008, she appeared in the **musical** *13* on Broadway.

Ariana considers 13 the show that gave her a start as an actress.

On Broadway

The **musical** *13* opened on Broadway in October 2008. Ariana had a small part as a cheerleader named Charlotte.

The musical is about a boy named Evan Goldman. His family moves from New York City, New York, to a small town.

Ariana (*front, second from right*) received a National Youth Theatre Associate Award for her work on *13*.

Broadway shows take place in certain theaters in New York City. They are considered to be some of the best shows in the country.

Lights! Camera! Action!

Ariana's work in *13* helped her get noticed. This led to other opportunities. In 2010, Ariana began acting on the Nickelodeon show *Victorious*. The show is about kids who attend a **performing** arts high school.

Ariana played Cat Valentine. Cat is known for being fun and sweet. She often dances and sings. This was an important step in Ariana's acting **career**. *Victorious* became one of Nickelodeon's most popular shows!

Ariana (*front, right*) was excited when *Victorious* won a Kids' Choice Award in 2012! It was for Favorite Television Show.

Ariana's acting **career** was growing. She played Cat on *Victorious* and *iCarly*. She also had other television parts. In 2011, Ariana began a voice **role** on the television show *Winx Club*. In 2013, she acted in the television movie *Swindle*.

Miranda Cosgrove was the star of *iCarly*. Ariana and Miranda became friends while working together on the show.

Break Out

Victorious came to an end in 2013. But in 2012, Ariana had gotten a lead **role** in Sam & Cat. This new show brought together stars from Victorious and iCarly.

In summer 2013, Sam & Cat **debuted**. It became very popular! Ariana continued playing Cat Valentine. Her costar was Jennette McCurdy. She played her iCarly character, Sam Puckett.

On *Sam & Cat*, Jennette and Ariana
are roommates and babysitters.

Pop Singer

Aside from being an actress, Ariana is a talented singer. She often sang **pop** music as part of her acting work. She was featured on three albums for *Victorious*.

In March 2013, Ariana **released** her own song, "The Way." It quickly became a hit. It was the first song from her album, *Yours Truly*. The album came out in September.

In November 2013, Ariana was named New Artist of the Year at the American Music Awards.

abc

AMERICAN MUSIC AW

In 2014, Ariana performed at the Billboard Music Awards.

A Performer's Life

As an actress, Ariana is very busy. She must practice lines for her **roles**. During filming, she works on a **set** for several hours each day.

As a singer, Ariana spends time writing and recording songs. She also practices **performing** them.

Fans are very excited to meet Ariana in person.

Ariana works hard to **promote** her shows and songs. She appears on television and in magazines. She attends events to meet fans. And, she **performs** live for audiences.

Off the Stage

Ariana spends free time with her family and friends. She enjoys reading Harry Potter books.
Ariana likes to help others. She helped start a singing group in Florida called Kids Who Care. It raises money for **charities**. Around 2009, Ariana traveled to South Africa to teach children music and dance.

Ariana has visited kids at Saint Jude Children's Research Hospital.

St. Jude Children's Research Hospital
ALSAC • Danny Thomas, Founder
Finding cures. Saving children.

27

Buzz

Ariana's talent as a singer and actress has won her many fans. She has thousands of followers on **social media** sites. *Sam & Cat* came to an end in summer 2014. But, fans are excited to see what's next for Ariana Grande!

Ariana won Favorite TV Actress at the 2014 Kids' Choice Awards. Actor Chris Rock and his daughter presented the award.

Snapshot

⭐**Name**: Ariana Grande-Butera

⭐**Birthday**: June 26, 1993

⭐**Birthplace**: Boca Raton, Florida

⭐**Appearances**: *13, Victorious, iCarly, Winx Club, Swindle, Sam & Cat*

⭐**Album**: *Yours Truly*

Important Words

career work a person does to earn money for living.

charity a group or a fund that helps people in need.

debut (DAY-byoo) to make a first appearance.

musical a story told with music.

perform to do something in front of an audience.

pop relating to popular music.

promote to help something become known.

release to make available to the public.

role a part an actor plays.

set the place where a movie or a television show is recorded.

social media a form of communication on the Internet where people can share information, messages, and videos. It may include blogs and online groups.

Websites

To learn more about Big Buddy Biographies, visit **booklinks.abdopublishing.com**. These links are routinely monitored and updated to provide the most current information available.

Index

Annie (musical) **8**

awards **13, 15, 21, 29**

Azalea, Iggy **23**

Butera, Edward **6, 26**

Carey, Mariah **9**

charity work **26, 27**

Cosgrove, Miranda **17**

Florida **6, 8, 10, 26, 30**

Garland, Judy **8**

Gillies, Liz **14**

Grande, Frank **7, 26**

Grande, Frankie **6, 7, 26**

Grande, Joan **6, 7, 26**

Grande, Marjorie **7, 26**

Heap, Imogen **9**

Houston, Whitney **8**

iCarly (television show) **16, 17, 18, 30**

Kids Who Care **26**

McCurdy, Jennette **18, 19**

New York **12, 13**

Nickelodeon **14**

Rock, Chris **29**

Sam & Cat (television show) **4, 18, 19, 28, 30**

South Africa **26**

Swindle (television movie) **16, 30**

13 (musical) **10, 11, 12, 13, 14, 30**

Victorious (television show) **14, 15, 16, 18, 20, 30**

Winx Club (television show) **16, 30**

Yours Truly (album) **4, 20, 30**